IMAGINE, BELIEVE AND BE:

The Blueprint for Creating your Life

Dean E Schaefer

First published by Dog Ear Publishing
4010 W. 86th Street, Ste H
Indianapolis, IN 46268
www.dogcarpublishing.net

ISBN: 978-159858-390-8

This book is printed on acid-free paper.

Printed in the United States of America

Acknowledgements

I would like to give thanks to the many people with whom I have crossed paths in my life. First and foremost, I would like to thank my parents, who have encouraged and inspired me throughout my life. I cherish your unconditional love and support that resonates in my heart as an eternal beacon of light. I also want to give a big thank you to my sisters Laura and Jeannie and my brother Bob. I have learned so much from each of you and have been able to lean on you, at different times and stages of my life that it makes it hard to express the blessing I feel having you in my life. I couldn't imagine my life without you. Thank you, I love you! To my children, Tayllor and Eric, thank you for everything you have given me. My spoken word is limited to the true meaning and love I have and feel for both of you. I have grown immensely as a spiritual being from the moment you entered my life. I love you both very much and I look forward to the many lessons you will continue to teach me. Thank you to my wife and friend, Renata. It is because of you, that this book is completed. Thank you for putting up with me while writing this book and keeping my grammar and spelling in 'Czech'. Thank you for your openness and for allowing me to bounce ideas off of you at all hours. Since our paths crossed, I have grown by leaps and bounds and I look forward to the many days of daily laughter we have ahead. Thank you again. I love you very much, you had me from hello.

I also give thanks to my close and dear friends and my incredible extended family; Jimbo, BoBo, BJ, Tracy, Terry, Jeralynn, George, Barbara (thank you for your time and effort on my first edit. I am grateful!) John, Reed, Jerry, Sonny, Doc M, Candy, Sandra, Debbie, Grandma Dood, Oli, Marti, Tim, Randy, Kelly, Timmy, Jessica, Brittanny, Cory, Landon and Miranda. Each of you has had an invaluable impact on my life and has helped (like it or not) to shape who I am today. I love you all very much!

Last but not least, thank you very much Linda Hines. Your expertise is greatly appreciated!

Contents

Foreword

Dean Schaefer has written a thoughtful examination of the way we act and react in our everyday lives and some variations on those processes that can improve the quality of our lives. He takes much of his thinking from Buddhist teachings which have been an effective model for living for millions of people for thousands of years.

For those people for whom daily life has become too complex and overwhelming and who have developed physical symptoms that reflect the frustration of their daily lives, Dean's recommendations may offer significant comfort. Dean worked as a massage therapist in my office for years, and he saw first hand how the frustrations and complications of living can literally "tie people up in knots." This writing may help to untie some of those knots for those willing to make the recommended changes.

Too often, people are unwilling to do what it takes to improve their own lives. Rather, they would prefer to take a pill or ask someone else to make the changes that would benefit them. For those who have reached a point in their lives when they know that change is necessary and they are willing to do the work, the ideas expressed herein can offer an effective blueprint toward a better and happier life.

Susan Meisinger, D.C., L.Ac.

Introduction

We are what we think. All that we are arises with our thoughts. With our thoughts, we make the world. —Buddha

You have complete control of your daily life experiences. You have the ability to create every minute of your life by how you think. It's that simple. I'll say it again. You can control your life experiences by how you think!

Through the ages we have forgotten this simple but important component of our spiritual essence. When we are unaware, our physical experience binds us and blurs our perception of what we are. We forget that our true essence is energy, pure energy, and we buy into the belief that our physical bodies are all we have. But that's not the case. We have a natural ability to create our lives by way of our thoughts, through energy.

The information presented in this book is based on my own experience of this profound but simple idea. I first became aware of this knowledge during my work as a bodywork therapist over the last 25 years (massage, neuromuscular therapy, cranial-sacral therapy, trigger-point therapy, and advanced energy healing).

As a working practitioner of the healing arts, I became conscious of this continuous energy field that we are made from and that connects us. I started to notice the correlation between how my clients felt and how they were thinking on any one day. It became clear to me that the more my clients talked of how bad their day was the more physical pain or discomfort they manifested. Likewise, the clients that maintained a more positive attitude exhibited far less pain expression. I also noticed that clients who expressed more negative thought energy tended to have more illnesses, sick or anxious animals, sick family members, and interestingly enough, difficultly in keeping their indoor plants green.

This basic awareness progressed and allowed me to start putting together the pieces of this amazing energy matrix that connects us. This ever-abundant source of energy is what I refer to as God Energy. God Energy is love, wellness, knowledge, and pure, ever-expanding creativity. Through my expanding knowledge of creative energy, I developed wisdom, knowing, and self-awareness. I learned that every experience I had and continue to have is directly created by my own thoughts. I now know I have complete control of any and all future experiences or desires I wish to create.

The God Energy referred to throughout this book is not the human form most of us have been taught to believe in. It is not a created image of the man who lives in the sky or some spiritual force that gets to decide if we are going to heaven or hell based on the choices we have made with our so-called dogmatic, free-will beliefs. No, the God Energy referred to here is the same energy force we all originated from before there was the physical "I" that we believe to be real.

God Energy is timeless, formless, has no boundaries, no labels and no judgments, and is part of everything we know to be. This God Energy is stillness, love, wellness, knowledge, and abundance that embraces everything and everyone. This God Energy constantly flows without fail. It knows nothing but pure creativity.

I use the label "God Energy" to allow for an easier identification and understanding of this magnificent creative energy source. This is the same energy source from which everything and everyone emanates and creates.

This God Energy has been labeled by many different cultures, religions and belief systems. God Energy has also been referred to as Universal Mind, Source Energy, Pure Spirit, Devine Intelligence, to name a few. We as physical incarnations identify with many labels of our own personal gods and beliefs. I mention these labels with great respect to the many different religions and belief systems available for each of us to seek and identify with, and within which we may practice our beliefs.

Unfortunately, the misunderstanding of this great God Energy has led to discontent among civilizations and countries throughout the planet's history. Because of this misunderstanding, mankind has created and witnessed many needless arguments, conflicts, and bloodshed.

When we remove our personal ego-driven thoughts about our gods and beliefs, we find the same common thread flowing through all of them and each of us. This common thread is love, wellness, and spirit. There is enough room in our boundless, ever-expanding universe to encompass each and every religion, belief, and god we worship. No person or group should assume they have a monopoly on anyone's unique spirituality or belief.

God Energy includes all gods and belief systems. It is pure love that emanates from the same source of creative energy where we all originate. This creative God Energy is not separate from who we are, it does not cast prejudice in any way, shape, or form. It embraces all believers and non-believers of every religion, creed, and culture. This God Energy is the life force of all mankind and the universe as we know it. It speaks to everyone individually, while binding us together as a whole. It encompasses every thing because of its intrinsic nature, which is our source of existence, our essence—God Energy.

It is meaningless to place a label on this energy source. It has no identity, no boundaries for our ego to claim. It just is. If you struggle with the label, God Energy, and feel the need to attach a different label, please use one that makes you comfortable and accepting of this energy. What we call it is not important here. What matters is your understanding that it's just energy, believing the principle is real, and accepting that we are all connected to it.

I have created my life and all of my experiences through this God Energy. Because of this, I am able to share my thoughts and beliefs on opening the door to your unique, self-created path to creating your life.

When the inspiration of this book flowed through me, I had no intention, or the know-how for that matter, to put my thoughts down in written form. If people had told me I would write a book about anything, I might have questioned their sanity. I have never considered myself a writer, nor would I have considered the idea of attempting to write a book.

I had no idea where this inclination, knowledge, or ability was coming from, but whatever the reason, I knew I had to put it down in book form. The thoughts and ideas entered my mind over and over as if I were being told by a higher source that this is what I will be doing, and that is exactly what was happening. It wasn't until I entered the pure, silent source of God Energy through meditation that I became aware this was the next phase in my development as a spiritual being. When I tapped into this awareness, the knowledge and organization truly started to flow through me. This is when the writing began.

Through this writing I hope to bring awareness to your innate and natural state of consciousness and your ability to create your world thought-by-thought. This natural state of consciousness is love, wellness, and an unlimited ability to create your life exactly as you intend it.

My goal is not to try and convince anyone of this innate knowledge or wisdom. My goal is to share and allow spirit to connect with this knowledge and flow as it will. If your spirit is open and your thoughts are right-minded, you can learn how to create the life you want and deserve, with ease, accuracy, and great abundance. Through this amazing, unlimited source of energy you can create health, happiness, knowledge, peace, relationships, or any physical form you desire. All you have to do is Imagine, Believe and Be.

With love, wellness and joy,
Dean Schaefer

I

Perspective and Learning to Think in the Right Mind

To enjoy good health, to bring true happiness to one's family, to bring peace to all, one must first discipline and control one's own mind. If a man can control his mind he can find the way to enlightenment, and all wisdom and virtue will naturally come to him. —*Buddha*

Remember the last time you felt blissful or joyous? I can guarantee at that moment, the moment you felt such happiness, you did not have one negative or judgmental thought roaming through your mind.

One of the first steps to thinking in the right mind and learning how to create your life is to stop old negative habitual thought patterns. Negative habitual thought patterns are the single most destructive thing we do as physical beings that stops us from obtaining what we truly desire in life. We label everything we interpret as good, bad, or indifferent. And when we label, we cast judgment, ultimately reflecting on how we feel about ourselves and our belief that we lack something in our lives. I have personally learned a great deal about this over the last several years. When I started to pay close attention to my thoughts and to becoming aware of present situations and experiences in my life, I realized the two were related. I started to experiment with reconditioning my thought patterns and side-stepping negative thoughts and began to see how I could create positive results in my life by changing my thinking. Through trial, I realized that when I changed my thoughts or perspective on my experiences, the results I experienced changed as well. This started an incredible journey and discovery of the true power we all harness, and the ability we all have, in creating our every experience, if we so desire.

I began this journey by becoming aware of the constant thoughts and perspectives on experiences appearing in my life. I started to pay close attention to the way I mentally reacted to what was happening in my day-to-day routine. When I became aware of my thoughts, I clearly saw when I felt judgmental or uncomfortable with certain situations, which allowed me to accept situations for what they were, without unnecessary judgment. I experimented with my thought choices and began to become aware of how uncontrolled and random those thoughts and perspectives could be. I realized I had a choice and could control how I reacted and felt about anything and everything I experienced.

STRESS

I once read there is no such thing as a stressful event or situation. An event or situation becomes stressful only when we attach an undesirable emotion to it, which we do by choice, every time.

It took me a while to absorb this statement and really understand it. This concept opened my eyes to the fact that I was in control of my reactions and feelings about any experiences. I began to grow an inner strength once I realized I had a choice. I no longer needed to allow an experience to dictate my emotional well-being. My awareness became more and more evident as this knowledge and understanding became clear to me. I began to understand how powerful my thoughts were, and how I perceived my world and the world around me.

I realized the so-called stress in my life was an illusion. It was simply a direct result of an undesirable emotion attached to a particular situation.

To give an example, we often hear people complain about their in-laws, how stressful it is when they come to visit, and how they can't wait until they leave. This undesirable feeling or emotion is directly related to a memory of a situation that no longer exists. The memory is entrenched because of a strong ego-consciousness and an unwillingness to release it.

When you choose to attach a negative emotion or memory to a particular situation, you create an active emotional volcano within yourself. This volcano, left unchecked, will spew destructive magma into your existence. The direct attachment of a negative emotion to memory causes you to react and believe an experience will be unfavorable.

The same situation for others can be a joyous occasion. How can the perception of the same situation be so opposing? It's not the situation or event that is stressful. It's the emotion you attach to the memory of it that provides the illusion of stress. And, if you believe stress is an illusion you create, then you have the power to choose your reaction. The choice is always yours to react positively or negatively to anything and everything in your life.

How do you do that? It all comes down to becoming aware, being present-minded, and being responsible for your reactions. When you stay present-minded, you take control of yourself and don't allow a memory to influence current reactions. By staying present-minded you allow every experience to be new and fresh and not bound by a memory.

We all know people who just cannot function when their home or environment is dirty or cluttered. They're the ones who ask you to remove your shoes before entering the house, and then they follow you around with a broom or feather duster. If something is out of place or not perfectly clean, they become anxious or angry. They can't seem to function if things are seemingly out of control in their environment.

Then there are people who can easily live with their house in complete disarray. They have a month's worth of dirty clothes lying around, dog hair covers the couch, and dirty dishes are piled up in the sink, as if these people are trying to set a balancing record for Guinness. Yet they are completely comfortable and calm with their surroundings. Different people react differently to their environment and it is the reaction that is either stressful or not.

Alleviate your stress by choosing your reaction to any given situation. Don't blame the situation. Be accountable for your reaction. Situations or events become cumulative perceptions that reside in your memory. When you attach negative emotions to them, you create a stressful predicament for yourself.

It is empowering to be aware and to know you can choose your emotion and reaction to any potentially stressful event or situation. By doing so, you change your experience and memory. When you bring awareness to this ability of choosing right-minded thoughts and emotions you reduce the illusion of stress.

DEALING WITH STRESS

Remember, stress is an emotion we attach to a memory of what we perceive happened. Empower yourself by choosing your perception and attaching an emotion that feels better.

1. Become aware of negative thought patterns and choose to change them.
2. Release the need to mentally label or judge any situation. Allow it to be as it is and focus your thoughts on what you want to experience. Labels and judgments are truly a game of self-competition played out in our minds using our egos as a referee.
3. Choose to 'feel' good regardless of your current perspective. Your emotional reactions are always a choice. It's the "feeling" aspect of your intended desire, how you emotionally feel, that attracts a matching vibration.

GET OVER IT

I heard a gem of wisdom on the radio one day that has helped me change my old negative thought patterns. It stated, "Once we get over ourselves, we can handle anything."

What a powerful statement! Once you remove your personal feelings about something, it goes away. When you put aside your ego and refuse to take offense to someone or something you are simply choosing to remove your personal feelings from the equation. You have taken the oxygen away from the fire. It can no longer burn you. You will no longer be offended and react to something in a negative way. Old negative thought patterns stop and an open perspective and opportunity to stay right-minded present themselves.

Let's say you are driving down the highway and a car in another lane zips by at a high speed then cuts into your lane and exits ahead of you. Most people would become angry, thus making it about them. They would take it personally. Next time this happens, instead of using expletives, allowing your ego to control your reaction, and becoming stressed, just remove your personal feelings about it. Say to yourself, "It's OK if I don't get to the freeway off-ramp before that car ahead of me." Or say something such as "That driver must need to be there before me."

Say anything, but don't allow the situation to become personal. No harm, no foul. By not allowing it to be a personal attack on you, and choosing to react with a right-minded response, you effectively remove a potentially stressful situation from your existence. It's like teaching the small child inside you not to throw a tantrum when things don't go your way.

Another opportunity to use this method of staying right-minded is when you make an appointment to see your doctor and, upon arriving, you have to wait longer than expected. Instead of choosing to become anxious and angry because you can't see the doctor at your scheduled time, remove your personal feelings and look for something positive. Say to yourself, "This gives me a little extra time," or "Maybe I can read or balance my checkbook while I'm waiting." Sometimes it's a great opportunity to stay in the moment and just be still.

Again, whatever the situation might be, just remove your sense of self from it and notice how much better you start to feel. You stay right-minded by simply removing your personal feelings from a situation or event and not allowing your ego to control you.

As a society, we need to quit taking life so personally and to stop looking for an opportunity to be offended. We all know people who seem to take everything personally. They don't seem to have much joy in their lives. They spit fire by blaming everyone around them for everything they experience, instead of looking within themselves to identify why they are creating their unpleasant circumstances.

Any time we choose to feel offended, we take away our positive, high-vibrating God Energy and replace it with a low-vibrating one, which we will label ego-conscious. Low-vibrating, ego-conscious energy is capable of creating every experience, just as high-vibrating energy is. And, even though it is negative in nature, it still emanates from the same source of creative energy.

If you allow these destructive low-energy thoughts to linger, they will manifest exactly the opposite of what you want. Once you're aware of how you feel about a particular situation or event, you'll gain the access and ability, the power over yourself, to choose peace and right-minded thoughts. With practice, you will keep yourself from falling back into old, negative thought patterns. You will immediately notice a dramatic difference in how you feel and act. You will also start to understand and feel that you are the creator of your life, and you do have control over anything and everything you desire and want to happen. You will become aware and understand it all starts with one thought at a time.

QUIT TAKING IT PERSONALLY

1. Don't allow yourself to become offended. When you choose to be offended you choose to be ego-conscious. Like the water on a duck's back, allow it to roll off.
2. Remove your personal feelings about an undesirable event and allow it to be. Controlling your personal feelings brings freedom and aligns you with positive creative energy.
3. Changing your perception to a positive vibration will always bring fresh and new experiences.

LOSE THE LABELS

Another method to help you condition a positive thought pattern is learning not to label and judge. Judgment is a destructive behavior we adopt once we have chosen to be offended. Our ego needs to justify why we are offended, and this always leads to some type of negative label. This type of reprogramming can be the most difficult to initiate, not because you want to judge, but because of a more embedded habit. In our society we tend to judge everything then we use these judgments to justify our existence and how we match up to our self-imagined competition.

You can learn to withhold judgment once you have understanding and sustained awareness. That will make an incredible difference in your life, as it has in mine. I learned that judging, like a mirror, reflects how I feel about myself. I judged everything and everyone for some reason or another, and most of the time I wasn't even aware I was doing it.

We all use judgments to make ourselves feel better about our insecurities. We use labels and judgments that reflect our thoughts and how we view our world such as "Those houses are ugly," "Those people think they're better than we are," "He thinks he's cool because he drives an expensive car," "He's an idiot," "She's fat," "Look at that (loser, dork, dweeb, nerd, redneck, hippie)." Use your imagination. The list goes on and on.

Every time you label and judge, you lower your spirit vibration and take two steps backwards and expose your fears and insecurities. When you are truly secure with yourself and have inner peace, which means you truly love yourself, you have no need to label or judge anything or anyone.

REMOVE YOUR PERSONAL FEELINGS

Our ego tells us if we believe someone or something is inferior to us, then we must be superior to it. When we allow this to happen, we give ourselves a false sense of security that feeds the ego. True creative God Energy has no ego. Tap into its infinite realm of love and wellness on a regular basis and your insecurities and need to cast judgment will melt away.

1. Observe, don't judge. Labeling and judgments are like giant mirrors reflecting an image of yourself. Allow all life expression to be as it is, without labels, without ego.

2. Love yourself. In the presence of love, the ego is lost. When you feel love, you are in the true presence of God Energy.

3. Play around with this and have some fun. Take notice how your life will start to change the moment you take control of your thoughts. Release your ego controlled thoughts and you'll live your life to the fullest.

4. Keep practicing. With continued practice, you will be able to choose right-minded thinking and bring sustained God Energy into every moment of your life. It is your choice and free will to do so. Impose your free will to create your life as you want it to be.

Once you internalize this, you will never need to spit fire again. You will know love, wellness, and peace—your natural state of being. You will be free to live and feel the bliss and joy of God Energy moment to moment in your everyday life. It is your right to do so.

There might be times when you'll slip back and find yourself caught up in your old negative thought patterns. It's OK. As soon as you become aware of negative thoughts, replace the label with something positive and let it go. Soon you will notice wonderful changes in your daily experiences. Life will become easy and fun, day by day, thought by thought.

SUMMARY

Incorporating these simple ideas into your daily experience will help you become calmer and more peaceful. Right-minded thinking will become natural for you. When right-minded thinking begins, you will see the first steps in creating your life, the life you want and deserve.

After the game, the king and the pawn go into the same box. You are not a King or a pawn, I am not a man or a woman, He isn't black or white, she isn't rich or poor. We are all god appearing, if you insist on a label, call it all magnificent. —Italian Proverb

II

Be Careful What You Ask For

Ask and it shall be given you, seek and ye shall find, knock, and it shall be opened unto you. —Matthew 7:7

Remember the expression, "Be careful what you ask for because you just might get it?" Well, I'm here to tell you it's true. I know you're probably saying, "Yeah, right," or you might be saying, "Well, it has happened a few times but not always." In either case, you have always received exactly what you asked for, no exceptions.

Upon closer examination of your thoughts and feelings, you will notice that you have always received exactly what you have focused upon. The challenge is that what you asked for is not usually what you were thinking about or feeling. How often have you said, "I didn't ask for this?" In fact, whatever showed up in your life was exactly what you thought about and felt.

The most powerful information you can harness is knowing that you create whatever you ask for and whatever you think about with emotion. This knowledge is the portal to how you create everything in your life.

We find it difficult to believe this is possible because when we ask for something, our minds recognize that we don't have what we are requesting. We ask because we believe or see ourselves as lacking or not having what we desire and want. We are mentally focused on the belief, "I do not have," and thus we create the "I do not have."

The key then to creating is to focus on what you want rather than on what you do not want. Most of us base our thoughts and beliefs on what we are experiencing in the present. The present, however, is a residual experience of past thoughts. We will not change a so-called undesirable experience by focusing on what we are currently experiencing.

The flip side of this is if you are enjoying your current experience, continue to focus upon the enjoyment and you will create more of it. Focus on what you want and stop focusing on what you do not want. If you are sick, do not focus on being sick. Focus your attention, with positive emotion, on being healthy and strong, as if it has already happened and you are currently enjoying its rewards. If you are worried about your finances you will create more of the same. Focus instead on what you want to create and forget about the current situation as a worrisome emotion. Focus on financial abundance, focus on the ideal situation you want to feel and experience. Keep it alive through belief. This is the way to creative freedom. No matter what the circumstance is, focus on what you want. Never give attention to or focus upon what you do not want.

God Energy does not know the notion "I do not have," or similar notions of deficiency. This energy does not discriminate either. It does not care if a thought is positive or negative from our perspective. God Energy creates only in our image, which is thought. When it comes to your desires and wants, God Energy will provide abundance. God Energy is everything, and everything is God Energy. We are all God Energy. We lack nothing. We just have to ask and believe!

You have the ability to create and experience anything you want or desire, as long as you believe. You emanate from the same energy field as everyone and everything else. There is no other source of energy. When you ask out of the lack for something, you get exactly what you are asking for, which is the lack of what you are trying to create. When you ask because you believe you are lacking something, you create exactly what you believe.

FOCUS ON WHAT YOU WANT, NOT ON WHAT YOU DON'T WANT

1. Be aware of what you are focusing on and the feeling you are attaching and reacting to. How you feel is always an indicator of the energy you are attracting.
2. Focus your attention and feeling on what you want. Do not focus on what is currently being perceived by your mind. Unless, of course, you would like to experience more of it.

3. Put your thoughts forward and create what you want. The current situation you are reacting to is simply a residual of past thoughts. Your current situation can only continue with sustained thoughts and expressed emotion of what is. Create anew by focusing all thoughts and emotion on what you want to experience.

When you ask for anything, believe that it is yours already, that you are enjoying and feeling it in the moment with positive emotion. Believe that no matter what, you have already received exactly what you asked for. Truly asking for something means truly believing you have already received it.

Understanding and knowing that you are an extension of creative God Energy helps you develop the belief that what you ask for has already arrived. Think of it as if you have seen your desire behind the curtain and you're just waiting for it to be revealed. Hold the feeling of anticipation and expect it to be, as if it already is. Think of the universe as your own endless and boundless warehouse holding every imaginable desire and belief. Visualize aisles of health, happiness, positive relationships, wealth, knowledge, and any physical form you can imagine. It's all there for you, as long as you ask and believe in your ability to obtain it.

To give an example, let's say you would like to have a specific car. You put your desire out there for the universe: "I want (model of car) and I want (color), with (options and equipment)." You've asked and some time goes by and you're still waiting and waiting. Doubt sets in and now you're saying, "I knew this asking and getting things doesn't work. I've asked for this car and I haven't gotten it."

Let's take a look at what you were probably thinking when you did the asking. Some thoughts may be, "I want this certain type of car but how am I going to afford it? There is no way I'll really get it. It would be nice to have, but I don't think it's possible."

Because of your true belief regarding the car of your desire, the mental erosion begins. Essentially what you have done is sabotage exactly what you were asking for. By thinking and believing negative thoughts, you have created what you were thinking about: "There is no way I'll really get it." And what do you have for asking? That's right, no car. You have just created what you actually asked for or, more precisely, thought and felt.

Words are just words until you put thought and emotion behind them. Once you do that you give your words intention. Intention mirrors or reflects your beliefs, and this reflection creates what you think and feel.

You have probably heard others say, "I never meet the right people. I always meet the ones who are wrong for me." These individuals are creating exactly what they believe and think. They bring these undesirable people into their existence, receiving what they asked for or what they were thinking about.

Remember, it's not the actual words spoken, but the intent behind the words that starts the creative process. The emotional thoughts and beliefs behind the words bring intention into play. And it is the true intent that creates your daily experiences. When you push against something you do not want, you create by default more of the same. It is this continual focus upon what you do not want to experience that forces you to experience it over and over.

ALLOW THE PRESENT MOMENT TO BE AS IT IS

1. Do not push against what is. Doing so will only create more of what is. By trying to push an unfavorable experience away, you are focusing upon it, thus creating more of what you do not want to experience.

2. Believe your desire is already in your experience. What ever your desire may be, you must act and believe as if you have already obtained it. Believing is seeing!

3 Feel and focus upon the anticipation. The feeling of anticipation is a powerful energy attractor and creator of vibration. Use it to your advantage, it's your right to do so.

4. Expect it to be, without exception. Belief, anticipation and expectation are powerful components of the creative formula for your desires.

No matter what your current situation might be, you cannot change what is at the moment. Allow and accept whatever you are experiencing and start focusing upon what you want. By focusing on what you want, you allow the present moment to be as it is. This allowing and awareness of present moment, attached with focus of what you desire, helps ensure the direct creation and experience of your life.

Have you ever noticed what goes through your head when you are starting to feel a little sick, perhaps a slight sore throat? You'll notice that you keep reaffirming to yourself that you have a sore throat. By telling yourself how sore and painful your throat is, you keep creating more of what you do not want, a painful sore throat. We actually create more pain by focusing on it. We keep it alive.

One night one of the dads on my son's baseball team seemed to be a little under the weather. I asked him if he was sick, and he replied, "Yes, but I usually don't get sick."

He told me that even if he starts to feel like he might be coming down with something, he'll usually tell himself he is not getting sick and it goes away. He shared with me a story of how he went fishing with some of his friends who were sick. He said as soon as he realized his friends were sick and they were sharing a cabin, he began to believe, "I'm definitely going to get sick being around these guys." He then said,

"That's exactly what happened, and now I'm sick because I told myself I was going to get sick."

This is a perfect example of how this entire process works. Because our thoughts and beliefs are so powerful, we are able to create what we think as long as we believe it to be true.

Have you ever had a pain somewhere in your body that seemed to go away briefly when you were not focusing on it? Maybe your thoughts were interrupted by a phone call. You realized after that, amazingly, you had no pain during that time. Your mind was occupied with something other than your pain, and you actually forgot about it.

YOUR MIND CREATES EVERYTHING YOU EXPERIENCE

The body by itself cannot create or interpret anything without thought, its spirit essence. A spiritless body cannot become ill without the ability to create thought. It cannot develop cancer, heart disease, mental illness, or anything else. Essentially, if a body without spirit is unable to think or focus, it is unable to develop a belief system and cannot create. But as soon as spirit enters a body your thoughts and beliefs control it. You can then create and control your physical life, including pain and illness, in any manner you choose.

If you investigate your thinking habits and patterns, you will be able to trace your thoughts to exactly this precise moment of your perceived existence. Where you stand today is the direct result of every single thought you have had in your life. It's a very powerful statement once you allow it to "be," and understand how it works. This knowledge gives you incredible control of the path you would like to walk while test-driving the physical body you have.

Have you ever had a desire or wanted something so badly that you knew it would "be" no matter what? You could see yourself doing exactly what you had planned or perhaps see the object of your desire, even though you didn't have it at that time. And then one day it showed up.

It is because you had a strong desire that held an undeniable belief behind it. You knew no matter what, you would have what you wanted. You saw yourself in your mind's eye enjoying your desired situation or object. Because of this strong belief, it put intention into motion, which ultimately led to your thought creation. It didn't show up by accident. Your steadfast thoughts and beliefs created it and brought it forth into your experience. This process echoes the Bible verse, "Thy will be done."

GIVE YOUR ASKING A STATE OF PRESENCE

Another component to consider when asking and creating is the manner in which you ask for what you truly want. It is important to structure your asking. For example, if you are creating health, you must not ask, "I don't want to be sick anymore." The word "sick" in your asking will always be sick, not feeling well. By focusing on the word "sick," regardless of your desire, you will create more sickness.

Focus instead on what you want. Say something along the lines of, "My body is healthy and strong. I want to continue feeling healthy and strong," and always finish by saying thank you. By saying thank you, you give your asking a state of presence, as if it has already occurred and you are expressing your gratitude.

The same method goes for any other type of desire. You will not create financial abundance if you are asking to be free of debt, because debt will always be debt. You cannot create a thin, healthy body if you are asking not to be fat anymore because fat will always be fat. And you cannot create knowledge if you ask not to be ignorant because ignorance will always be ignorance. Again, focus on what you want, not on what you do not want.

1. If you want health, choose to "feel" healthy and act and believe as if you truly are healthy.
2. If you want happiness, choose to "feel" happy and act and believe as if you truly are happy.
3. If you want prosperity, choose to "feel" prosperous and abundant and act and believe as if you are.
4. The "feeling" of any desire is always in direct relation to your vibrational output and what you are attracting into your experience. Whatever your desire might be, you must truly "feel" it, "be" it, and "believe" it will be, no matter what.

SUMMARY

It is important to understand how you create your life and how careful you must be when asking for anything you desire or want. Take a moment and look around. Everything that surrounds your daily experiences started with a simple desire or want. It was then followed by a belief, known or unknown, that caused it to appear in your experience.

The blueprint for your life requires only a desire or want followed by an undying belief to create it. If these two components are in place, you will be able create and live your life as if you wrote the script.

As a man think in his heart, so he is. —*Proverbs 23:7*

What we think, we become. —*Buddha*

III

High and Low Energy,
After All, It's Just Energy

"Energy is the only thing I know to be constant."—- *Unknown*

Everything emanates from energy. Energy is what gives form to every physical and nonphysical thing we perceive in our world and is the building block of all creations to be. Our bodies are energy. Our cars are energy. Our houses are energy. Our families are energy. Our currency is energy. Our thoughts are energy. Our emotions are energy. Everything we label as something is energy. Even energy is energy.

One of the most overlooked aspects of energy is that we can change and manipulate it at any time, with ease. Understanding this principle gives you great power and control to shape and create life, the life you want and deserve.

You have the ability to create your life moment to moment when you understand that energy is not static, that it is constantly moving and changing. Everything you see, touch, or even think about is a form of energy materializing out of nothingness. You can find this information in any quantum physics workbook.

In short, quantum physics is the study of matter on a subatomic level. The study of quantum physics reveals just how bizarre and wild our perceived reality can be. I have read only the basic principles of quantum physics, which works for my understanding of what I'm presenting here. Many books and learning materials are available for anyone who would like to do some serious reading on the subject. Understanding quantum physics helps you see how you can begin to create your desired life.

First, you must understand that any physical or nonphysical manifestation and belief you perceive is simply a group of tiny energy particles. When you break these tiny energy particles down, you find more of the same. Each sequential breakdown of these particles reveals smaller and smaller units of energy. The cycle continues until you reach a realm of nothingness. It is from this realm of nothingness that everything is created.

For example, let's look at a steel beam used to build a bridge. At first glance, we believe this steel beam is a solid static object not capable of moving. But if we look at it with an electron microscope, we get a better picture of what it really is.

An electron microscope reveals the steel beam to be made up of molecules bouncing off one another. From there, if we increase the magnification, we notice these molecules are made up of atoms, and these atoms are bouncing off one another as well. With increased magnification we notice the atoms have particles called protons, neutrons, and electrons. Electrons magnified show particles within called quarks, and in the quarks we would see leptons, gluons, baryons, and mesons. It just keeps going. The empty area around these tiny particles and the particles themselves are 99.999 percent pure empty space, or nothingness.

It is from this pure empty space that all life and creations emanate. It is at this level of pure spirit that we find the unlimited source of love, wellness, and God Energy. An abundance of pure, creative spirit is all that exists at this level, which is set into motion with a simple pure, creative thought.

I used a steel beam in this example, but you can take any matter and break it down to the same sub-atomic level and net the same results. It breaks down to the same pure empty space or nothingness, no matter what physical object it appears to be. The scenario is the same if we look at our thoughts.

Although we cannot see or feel our thoughts, they are a form of expanding energy that can be monitored and measured as brain activity. Sensitive medical and scientific frequency devices can measure our thoughts as frequency, and energy is a frequency. Because of this we know our thoughts are units of physical energy, and physical energy can always be dissected or broken down to the level of stillness or nothingness, the origin of all creation. This phenomenon reveals the connectedness of everything and everyone. It points to the simple conclusion there is no other creative source field.

You cannot find anything in your physical or nonphysical experience that breaks down to anything other than pure, creative energy, God Energy. We share the ability to create our lives in any manner desired because we are all created from and are connected to this source. Understanding this basic concept reinforces the constant connection we maintain with each other and all things. We are all the same.

Quantum physics tells us we all break down to the same source field of creative God Energy. It does not matter what our culture or our race is or what demographic label is attached to us. We all have the same access to this infinite realm of love, wellness, and abundance.

This infinite field of creative stillness is our true source, our essence. There is no reason for any physical form to be without love, wellness, and abundance. You cannot be separate or different from what you are. You are God Energy, and God Energy is all there is. A simple thought and belief, positive or negative, will set forth and initiate the powerful law of creation.

HARNESS YOUR FREE WILL TO CREATE YOUR LIFE AS YOU DESIRE

Our thoughts are pure, creative energy. You did not manifest into your current physical form only to suffer or lack for anything. Your free will allows you to create your experience.

1. Use the power of positive thinking attached to a strong positive emotion to manipulate your attracting energy. The universe does not discriminate when it comes to vibration. It reacts to every impulse—positive or negative. Remember, positive in, positive out—negative in, negative out. Focus your thoughts forward, do not focus on what is currently happening. Believe and feel

your desire. It's just energy, play with it and have fun.

2. Funnel your thoughts to create your desired reality. Every thought is an energy pulse ready to create. You can sculpt your energy vibration with pinpoint accuracy, like a laser-pointer, using your thoughts and emotions as a directional compass pointing the way to your tangible creation.

SUMMARY

You have the gift and ability of individual thought choice. As a spiritual being, you are capable of creating whatever you desire. If you are aware of the thoughts you generate, you will better understand your innate creative nature. Your constantly expanding thoughts create your life.

When you allow and understand that we are all connected to the same creative energy source, a new and wonderful opportunity will unfold every moment a thought is born. With each intended thought, you learn to create and form your life expression, as you will, as you desire, through God Energy. After all, it's just energy.

"Energy is everything and everything is energy." — *Unknown*

IV

Raising your Energy Level

You, yourself, as much as anyone in the entire universe, deserve your love and affection. —*Buddha*

It is important to understand the concept of energy because of a powerful force called the Law of Attraction. The Law of Attraction states, "That which is like itself is drawn unto itself." This law shows us that a positive high-vibrating energy draws to itself a positive high-vibrating energy. The same principle applies for a negative low-vibrating energy. We can give and receive in life only that which we are. The old saying "misery loves company" is not just some random quote. It truly follows the Law of Attraction. It's the same idea when we hear a comment such as "likes attract," or "what goes around comes around." These are all statements that have been touted for years and years, and they all detail the Law of Attraction.

Try to imagine yourself as a magnet pulling into your experience a creative vibrational energy that matches your current emotion. Every thought and feeling you choose generates this creative vibrational energy and creates your daily life experience. For example, every time you choose to carry a negative vibration such as hate, you create hate into your experience. And every time you choose to carry a positive vibration such as love, you create love in your experience. The Law of Attraction shows you how you are truly feeling about anything and everything.

The magnet analogy is perfect because we are all energy magnets. We attract energy vibrations with each and every thought and feeling. They guide the Law of Attraction. Our emotions are the internal indicator or meter of what experiences we are creating at any given moment. This is why you must attach a positive emotion to a desire. It is the emotion— the feel-good state of presence—that assures you create something positive into your experience. The old adage, "Follow your emotions because emotions don't lie," could not be more precise.

The emotion you attach to a situation tells you if you are vibrating either on the high positive side or on the low negative side of your internal meter. By understanding "it's just energy," you can begin to change your vibration. Pay attention to the emotions attached to a thought. This can instantly change the thought vibration you are creating. It can mean the difference between experiencing a desire or something undesired.

You begin to realign with your true desires and your creative source by becoming aware of your emotional offering at any moment. When this happens, the door will open and allow you to take the first steps in the creation of your life experiences.

CREATE YOUR DESIRED EXPERIENCE

1. Imagine yourself as a magnet attracting a matching vibration. With every thought and feeling pulling towards your experience a matching vibration.
2. Become fully aware of your emotional offering. Your emotions are your vibrational offering. Make sure you're aware of how you "feel" when deliberately creating.
3. Focus on feeling good. It is the "feeling" that creates your experience. When focusing on feeling good, by default, you automatically create more of what you are feeling good about.

RAISE YOUR ENERGY VIBRATION

You have the unlimited ability to change and raise your energy vibration to one of positive creation if you understand and know how the Law of Attraction works and how your emotions guide it. At this point of understanding and awareness you will then attract the positive, high-vibrating energy of your choosing. When you are aware of your emotions, you instantly know the set point of your internal creative vibration meter.

You maintain positive energy levels when you start to recognize your emotions. Happiness, optimism, excitement, exhilaration, enthusiasm, joy, bliss, and love are examples of positive, high-vibrating energy. Sadness, anger, jealousy, resentment, anxiety, grief, hate, and fear are examples of low-vibrating energy. These energies are not listed in any ascending or descending order. They are listed randomly for identification purposes. Your ability to identify a particular emotion or feeling at any one time is a powerful tool in becoming a deliberate creator of your experience.

Once you are aware of your feelings and emotions, you can then choose a reaction that keeps you in vibrational harmony. When you choose to live in vibrational harmony on a regular basis, you keep your creative channels open and clean. By doing this, you will see a quicker manifestation of your wants and desires, with greater abundance and accuracy.

CHOOSING GOOD VIBRATIONS

It is easy to stay in tune with your vibration harmony just by becoming aware and staying present-minded. The majority of your thoughts are concentrated on past events that cannot be changed or on a future you create in your mind that does not exist. The only thing that is real is this moment, and even that is open for discussion.

You can create your life only in the present moment, by seeking the abundance of good that surrounds your life each and every moment. Nothing has ever happened in the past or the future. Everything happens in the present moment. We have all heard the phrase, "Be thankful for what you have, rather than dwell on what you don't have," or, better put, "what you think you don't have."

The Law of Attraction bears out this statement. By aligning your energy vibration with your desires, you can manifest what you give your attention to or what you are seeking.

A good way to start raising your energy vibration is by simply being thankful and gracious. This can mean many things to many people. It encompasses appreciation, gratefulness, realization, sensitivity, admiration, love, and acknowledgement.

To create a good, positive vibration, dedicate fifteen minutes a day to becoming aware and being thankful for all the good surrounding your life. You will find your thankfulness in the simplest of things that you might overlook on a daily basis. For example, the next time your alarm clock goes off to start your day, say something such as "I am thankful for my alarm clock. It allows me to wake up on time every morning."

You might think this is silly, but by doing this you are choosing to shift your mental viewpoint into a positive vibration. This helps you avoid the negative vibration that sometimes occurs upon being awakened by the alarm clock.

Continue to be thankful for everything you want to experience more of, even if it seems to be insignificant. Be thankful for your toothbrush because it helps you keep your teeth clean and your hairbrush because it untangles your hair and your seatbelt because it keeps you safe. Do you see the pattern here? It doesn't matter what it is or how insignificant it might seem, just be thankful for it. The genuine act or thought of being thankful automatically raises your energy vibration, allowing for more of the same to manifest itself.

You can find thankfulness and appreciation in a seemingly negative situation too. If your workload or family life is stressful, you can still find the abundance of good if you allow yourself. A positive viewpoint when things seem difficult might be, "Even though my present situation seems overbearing, I know it's temporary, and I'm learning from it," or, "I will continue to grow from this experience. It is getting better every moment," or, "I am thankful that I know I will gain control of this situation and overcome it."

All it takes to change a negative situation into an opportunity for positive and deliberate creation is knowing and believing that a situation is temporary and that it is getting better every moment.

When faced with an adverse situation in which you find nothing to be thankful for, be thankful that you have the awareness to know that the particular experience does not feel good and that you would like it to change. Your awareness of any negative energy will start to change it and replace it with a higher energy vibration. Even though you might have a hard time being thankful at times, it's the awareness of how you are feeling that starts the process of raising your vibration.

When you bring a bad feeling to awareness, or into light, you are acknowledging that it does not feel good and this allows you to begin focusing on what you want. When you decide what it is you want, by default you will start to create it, as long as you focus on what you want.

Sometimes we are faced in life with what seems to be an "impossible to change" state of mind. This could be the result of a relationship, an injury to you or someone you care for, or any number of tragic or possibly life-threatening situations. In this case, it might be helpful to focus upon an image from your past or someone you love that conjures a positive feeling you can embrace. By focusing on the positive feeling of thought, a seemingly negative experience can begin to heal and turn for the better.

As long as you exude positive energy and harmonious thoughts, you are moving in the right direction. If you continue in the right direction, you will move up on your energy scale and reach your goal. The Law of Attraction has no other choice but to align with your vibrational match.

Do not expect to change years and years of negative thoughts overnight. Raising your vibration level is a cumulative process that is neither rapid nor dramatic. If you stay constant in your vision to change your vibrational output, you will begin to realign with your positive, creative self, and you will always reach your goal. You must believe before you will see.

STAY CONSTANT IN YOUR VISION

1. Say thank you! Showing and feeling gratitude is one of the greatest positive vibration attractors. Truly feeling grateful is always in direct alignment to God Energy. Appreciation and gratitude is always reciprocated.
2. Raise your vibration. It's as easy as changing your socks. Decide what color you want and wear it. Feeling good or feeling bad is always a choice. How do you want to feel today?
3. Feeling good, feeling joy, is really what life is all about. We are all motivated by our desires to ultimately feel good and joyous. Life is good, have fun!

SHOW LOVE AND LEARN FORGIVENESS

When it comes to ourselves, we often forget to be kind, loving, and forgiving. You can give only what you are. To raise your energy vibration, be kind to yourself and others. Showing love, kindness, and forgiveness to yourself is as simple as saying that you like and love who you are. You can also do nice things for yourself such as going shopping for something you've had your eye on or treating yourself to a special indulgence that brings you peace and joy. Whenever you feel peace and joy you know you are vibrating with the highest God Energy possible.

Another way to raise your vibration level is by learning to forgive. This can be quite challenging for many. As I mentioned in Chapter One, finding reasons to forgive can be as easy as not taking things personally. If you harbor resentment toward someone or something, it is best not to take it personally and not to look for reasons to be offended.

It is a lot easier to be peaceful than to be right and worried about being offended. If you decide to take the stance of being right you give strength to your ego and weaken your creative power. The need to be right is a futile attempt by the ego to establish itself and gain superiority over simple thought form that has no meaning or credence. Resentment is a big energy attractor and you are an energy magnet. The quicker you learn to control your ego and forgive, the quicker you'll move up the energy meter.

Anything that has happened to you is in the past. It cannot be changed in any way, shape, or form. It does not matter if you replay the scenario in your head over and over. It cannot be undone. When your bruised ego will not let things go, you stay at a negative energy level with no resolution. Don't attach your personal self to the situation. It no longer exists. Acknowledge it, take it as a lesson learned, forgive, and let it go. Don't give your ego life by reliving a memory that no longer exists and projecting into a future that is not real. Once you learn to take control of yourself and not let your ego control you, you will start to live in the present moment where you can create a life of love, driven by pure God Energy without fear. Your ego cannot exist if you live in the present moment and live with forgiveness.

Forgiving is the most powerful and dramatic action you can take if you wish to be a deliberate creator of your life. When you forgive you are forgiven.

The ability to forgive has nothing to do with a particular situation or person. It has everything to do with your own forgiveness and love of yourself and how well you are connected to God Energy.

Forgiveness is pure love, and the only thing standing between you and pure love is your ego. When you hold grudges, you hold yourself hostage from a beautiful, creative universe. Remember, you create what you focus on, and grudges hold an incredible amount of emotion.

We all know what it's like to see a small child misbehaving in a public place. Your ego is like that child, kicking and screaming if things don't go its way. Why would you allow that misbehaving child to live within you and disrupt your home?

Once you have learned to be kind to yourself, you can then extend kindness and love to others. When you do this, the Law of Attraction will always reciprocate. There is no other direction for the Law of Attraction to flow. You will reap what you sow.

Take a few moments throughout your day and give out what you would like to receive. Say hello to a complete stranger or ask someone if they would like help with something. When somebody says to have a nice day, reply, "Thank you, I will. You have a nice day too." It is amazing how good it feels to extend true kindness to another person and how wonderfully easy it becomes. We have all heard the phrase, "Perform random acts of kindness," but how many of us actually do it? When you do this, your vibrations elevate instantly to a level of pure creation.

Give more hugs. The act of showing love and affection is truly the greatest gift you can give and receive. We all know how wonderful it feels to receive a genuine, love-felt hug. Go ahead and treat yourself.

Don't be so hard on yourself. Let your mantra be "I am doing the best I can with what I know, and everyday I am learning more and more." This is exactly what everyone else is doing. When you realize that, you relieve a lot of pressure. Your responses are based upon the ability and knowledge you have acquired up to the present moment.

We all have different paths to walk and are all on different journeys. Each and every one of us will grow, learn, and become enlightened at our own chosen moment. You might not agree with someone, but that simply signals different perceptions based on knowledge or experience you've each acquired up to that moment. It is the emotion you attach based on a memory you have had that allows you to experience the same situation differently. Your experience of a situation may differ completely from someone else's. The sooner you adjust your thinking to a positive direction, the sooner you will be able to handle challenges in your experience.

Practice the art of not using labels or judgments and loving the child within. When I was in high school, a teacher said to me, "Treat yourself like the child you would love." This statement is beautiful and pure. If you practice this statement, you will truly love yourself.

FACTORS THAT INFLUENCE YOUR ENERGY VIBRATION

I know a lot of people who allow the media, whether it is printed or on television, to influence how they see and feel about their current life situation. It is truly tragic to see how this mainstream brainwashing so easily influences people. When people read or hear about how bad the economy is or how many people were killed in their neighborhood it can skew their beliefs.

Avoid being influenced by focusing on your own unique bubble rather than on the collective human bubble. As soon as you focus on what you want, you will start to attract the life you want, not one the media creates. Remember foremost when watching TV or reading the newspaper, the media is in the advertising business. They use anything they can to grab your attention and sell ad space. Unfortunately, most of the time they feature sensationalism or fear, which creates more fear.

If you allow yourself to think and believe the world you see through the media is the only choice you have, you will create more fear-based experiences into your reality. I'm not suggesting you shouldn't watch TV or read the paper, but be aware and understand the true source of the information. Exercise discretion with your emotional response to what you view.

Be open, and do not let outside sources contaminate your energy. You are the creator of your experiences and you have the power to choose your thoughts and reactions regardless of what you hear or read.

CHOOSE YOUR FRIENDS WISELY

If you truly want to improve your vibration, choose to keep people close who resonate in a high-positive vibration. When you allow a low-energy vibration to filter into your environment, you cause a chain reaction of contaminated, low vibrating energy to overtake your positive, high vibrating energy because it is difficult to maintain a high-vibrating creative energy in the presence of a low-energy creator.

Everyone has different reasons for allowing certain vibrations to co-exist in their environment. Remember, though, you are an energy magnet. If you are drawing low-vibrating energy to you, please reevaluate your choices and be cognizant of which direction you are heading on your vibration scale.

It is a kind gesture to help those who seem to be in a bad place. Sometimes, though, as hard as it might be, you have to allow people to find their own way. This does not mean you cannot care for or continue to love them. It simply means it is important that you do not allow their low vibration to consume or contaminate your energy.

Don't take others' challenges as your own or make them personal to you. Everybody makes their own choices and creates their own experiences in life, no exceptions. We all choose our own paths to walk for whatever reason. No matter how down and out someone might appear, they have created their experience with their thoughts.

We can feel each others' energy. Some people broadcast their emotional state loud and clear. Typically, these people make you uncomfortable, uneasy, anxious, or even fearful just by being in their presence. Have you ever noticed the feeling of energy when walking into an environment where people have been arguing? You immediately feel a heavy sensation without even knowing the circumstances. This sensation is your sensory awareness coming into play, and it presents itself immediately.

This awareness is your emotional guidance system. It allows you to feel energy signals, good or bad. Tapping into this awareness gives you instant feedback as to the type of energy that is present. If you are exposed to negative energy for a long time, eventually it will contaminate your energy field and may start the process of creating an undesired experience.

Be aware of how energy makes you feel so you can immediately choose to feel good at any time. Don't let someone else's negative energy contaminate yours and damage your vibration.

This same sensory awareness is apparent with people who resonate a high-positive vibration. These are people you feel comfortable with regardless of any shared history. The first time you meet them you feel as if you have known them your entire life. You feel good when you're with them or even thinking about them because they create positive energy. You will want to allow them into your experience.

Surrounding yourself with these people helps you keep your vibration high and pure, and you will feel it moving in the right direction on your internal energy meter. You will create your own defining circle. It will be you, and it will be one of positive creation.

INCREASING YOUR POSITIVE ENERGY VIBRATION

1. Every couple of days, increase by a couple of minutes your allocated time of thankfulness, appreciation, kindness, forgiveness, and love. Before you know it, with continued practice, it will become effortless and natural.

2. Become conscious daily of the energy you create, and the energy that you allow into your life experiences. Do not allow any outside forces to comtaminate your clean and pure creative pond.

3   Monitor your media intake and be aware of your reaction. It's ok to stay informed as long as you do not allow yourself to become inundated with the negative gimmick of news and entertainment broadcasting. Focus your thoughts on what you want to experience, not on what is being shown to you. Keep your bubble crystal clear and make it your own.

4. Choose to keep positive company. Do not allow your self to get caught up in the drama of someone else's life. Holding a high positive vibrational resonance will always ensure matching relationships.

5. Hug someone. ☺

SUMMARY

You will find with time and practice, that the creation of positive energy becomes effortless and fun. You will also realize and reap significant and positive benefits in your overall daily experiences.

You will become a direct conduit for the Law of Attraction by keeping your vibration high and pure. This will bring positive high-vibrating energy and experiences into your daily life, moment to moment. You will then become aware that you are the creator of your life.

Judge not, that ye be not judged. For with what judgment ye judged; and with what measure ye mete, it shall be measured to you again. —*Matthew 7:1,2*

Those who are free of resentful thoughts surely find peace. —*Buddha*

V

Imagination and
the Art of Visualization

The true sign of intelligence is not knowledge but imagination. Imagination is everything; it is the preview of life's coming attractions. —
Albert Einstein

Imagination is the ability to create any thing or any circumstance in your mind. It is the foundation of thought creation. At some point in our physical development we, unfortunately, are discouraged from using it. Do you remember your grade school teachers telling students to stop daydreaming? Those who continued to daydream were reprimanded and received unfavorable marks on their report cards. Even in adulthood, it seems society labels daydreamers as different or immature.

Because of instilled sociologic beliefs that daydreaming is an undesirable activity for anyone over the age of eight, we have forgotten it is part of our innate creative nature. This makes us a little afraid to engage in daydreaming on a regular basis.

Some people believe that imagination and visualization are the same thing. In fact, imagination and visualization invoke the same principles, but they are two different steps of the same desired outcome. Imagination is the creative thought, or series of thoughts, that start the whole process of creation. As Einstein said, "It's the preview of life's coming attractions." It is a tiny seed planted in the stillness of God Energy that causes a ripple in the pond of creation. From that ripple, the seed of thought starts to take vibrational form and aligns with our emotional frequency. This starts the creation process because a thought was born, and we begin to use the power of visualization. When you visualize, you put your imagined thought into motion and bring it alive in your mind's eye. Imagination and visualization walk the same intertwined line. Both are important and powerful components of our creative process.

We should all imagine and visualize our desired experience of reality on a daily basis. Unfortunately, most of us never learned and realized how powerful and creative this gift is, and how innate and automatic it is. We often create experiences that we do not want because of the lack of awareness regarding this built-in knowledge. If you take a close look, you will notice how it all ties into "Be careful what you ask for," or, as I like to say, "Be careful what you think about."

We visualize or fantasize about different aspects of our lives, including some of our greatest fears. We daydream or fantasize about going on vacation, making lots of money, having dinner with somebody, or being at work and facing certain situations. We also replay conversations we have had, will have, or think we might have, over and over until we wear them out. We tend to imagine and visualize things we would never want to happen such as illness and accidents. We imagine tragedies such as our being stuck in a fire, experiencing an earthquake, being assaulted by somebody, and suffering other unpleasant scenarios. I don't know why we conjure these images, but we all seem to do it repeatedly until one day one of these images manifests and we wonder how something like that could happen to us. It's important to remember that when we unconsciously or consciously participate in any type of visualization, we tend to attach emotion to it, and it's the emotion that carries with it the vibration of creation, positive or negative.

The great thing about the gift of imagination and visualization is that we can, at any time, choose to create an image with a positive vibration and emotion attached to it. When you are aware of this you can recognize when you are seemingly locked into a negative thought pattern, and work to change your vibration to a positive direction.

POSITIVE VISUALIZATION

Take about ten minutes a day and practice this amazing principle. Find a quiet area that feels comfortable and live your desire through your mind's eye.

1. Create an image or circumstance you would like to experience. This created image must be clear and direct. This is where "Be careful what you ask for" comes into play. Be as detailed as possible to create your desired outcome.

2. Attach a strong, positive emotion to that which you desire. See yourself as already having attained your desires. Visualize your desired outcome or the end result you wish to experience. Act and believe as if it has already happened.

3. Visualize yourself walking the path that leads you to your wants or desires or visualize yourself standing at the end of your desired outcome, at the finish line, watching yourself arrive. Either way you do it, feel and embrace the positive emotions to create your desire.

4. Live and experience your dreams in the moment. Act out your own melodrama with intensity. Life is your stage. Earn an Oscar.

FROM POSITIVE VISUALIZATION TO POSITIVE VIBRATION

Be aware of how you will feel once you create your desire. Take hold of that feeling, then attach to the feel-good emotion you have created. Attach it to your desired result. It is the feel-good emotion you need to become aware of and harness. By doing this, you are choosing and creating your vibration harmony and aligning with what you desire. You activate the Law of Attraction when you bring awareness to your feel-good vibration and hold that aspect. And because the Law of Attraction is "That which is like itself is drawn unto itself," you will be a perfect match to create and receive your desire.

The more often you hold and embrace a positive vibration, the more you will start to resonate as that created vibration. When your being resonates and radiates a particular vibration, you attract experiences of like vibration. Feel the excitement and the wonderful anticipation of your wanted desire and hold it as if it has already arrived. This is where expectation comes into play.

FROM POSITIVE VIBRATION TO EXPECTATION

Harness the feeling of expecting your desire. The expectation of something to come is a very powerful energy attractor. In light of this, it is important to feel and hold this component of creation. When you expect something, and you strongly believe it will be there, you will create it. Whatever it might be, visualize yourself doing it, feeling it, anticipating it, experiencing it with excitement and you "will" it into your existence.

Imagination and visualization are powerful gifts we all possess. Have fun with them. Fantasize without limitations or boundaries. Create an image or circumstance with a strong positive emotion attached to it, embrace the feeling of it, and you'll create it. Create the belief and create your life.

Everything we see and perceive is a direct result of a belief that it will be. Endless opportunity exists in the realm of creation if we use our gift of imagination. Think of the technologic advancements and marvels that have taken place throughout our history, or all of the so-called miracles that take place in people's lives on a daily basis. Nothing happens by accident. Everything is created by our thoughts and through this powerful creative ingredient of imagination. The possibilities are limitless when you think about the positive changes that can transpire through the power of your imagination.

SUMMARY

We are all secure with what is known, what is safe. It takes imagination and visualization to explore the unknown.

This new and uncertain field of the unknown offers unlimited opportunity and growth as a spiritual being. From this field of the unknown, you have a chance to do and experience things that you have not yet discovered. Embrace your imagination and your ability to visualize, for every morning you awake, you have an opportunity to create joy and a chance to experience the unknown.

Imagination is more important than knowledge. For knowledge is limited to all we now know and understand, while imagination embraces the entire world, and all there ever will be to know and understand.
—Albert Einstein

Where there is no vision, the people perish. —Proverbs 29:18

VI

Believing Is Seeing

Faith is the substance of things hoped for, the evidence of things not seen. —Hebrews 11:1

What we are today comes from our thoughts of yesterday, and our present thoughts build our life tomorrow: our life is the creation of our mind. —Buddha

We have all heard the phrase, "Seeing is believing." If we embrace this idea then we must believe that anything is not possible. The true foundation of creation is based on your ability to believe that something is possible even if you have no evidence of it at the present moment. But, turn it around and you have, "Believing is seeing."

What is believing? It is a parallel energy to faith and is the main component to manifesting all of your desires. True believing is also the releasing of any fears you might have. Believing is inner knowing and confidence. It's an absolute. Believing orchestrates the energy of intention and leads it to creation.

When we believe in something, we are in true creation harmony. We walk the walk, we talk the talk.

Have you ever noticed that truly confident people are often successful in acquiring what they want? These people are sometimes labeled as arrogant or overly confident. Regardless, they are able to tap into the realm of creation and manifest most anything they desire. Why is this? True confidence is born from believing in yourself and your ability to obtain anything you set your mind to do. Confident people believe anything they desire is attainable. Their strong belief overrides any fear or doubt that might hinder them in their quest.

When you truly believe in something, you have the ability to create your experience the way you want to experience it, with great abundance. True belief is free of fear and doubt. Believing is seeing allows for the absolute abundance of all things possible and not yet known.

Become aware of your belief system and you will understand how it affects your experiences. The challenge is our beliefs don't necessarily jump out in front of us to announce, "Hey, this is how I believe!" Many times we are not aware of our own true beliefs. This simple unawareness then allows us to create undesirable circumstances into our experiences.

Every experience is created by way of our thoughts, and is always related to how we believe. This is why paying attention to your emotions plays such an important role in your creations.

EMOTIONS SIGNAL BELIEF

Your emotions are a direct result of how strongly you believe in a particular situation or circumstance. When you are happy, you believe things are good. When you are sad or fearful, you believe things are bad at that moment. When you pay close attention to your emotions, you can become aware of your beliefs. This awareness of your emotions and beliefs allows you to navigate your thoughts into creation.

Some of our beliefs are not necessarily based on our own experience. We tend to believe in things without knowing why. Sometimes we have no knowledge or experience of things we believe. We have formed a belief based on someone else's experience and interpretation. This type of belief system can be destructive when you are trying to create your life. You may hold onto your parents' or friends' beliefs, for example. It is only when you take notice and become aware that you can begin to re-evaluate your beliefs, without prejudice, and shape your life.

How many times have you disliked someone you've had no prior experience or personal interaction with because a friend or a family member had an unfavorable experience with that person? This borrowing of belief systems is evident in all aspects of our lives, from politics, religion, philosophy, childrearing, diet, nutrition, automobiles—you name it. You've probably borrowed your belief about it at one time or another.

Remember, there is no such thing as a stressful situation or event. It is only the emotion you attach to it that can make it stressful and can determine how you experience it. The emotion you generate carries your belief, and the emotion you attach to a situation or thought invokes the Law of Attraction. Like experiences then align with your vibration. This is why it is very important to keep your belief systems your own, based exclusively on your experiences and not on those of others. By doing this you ensure that your energy vibration stays in the positive creation aspect and does not become contaminated with others' negative experiences. It also allows your unique experience of any situation and prevents you from drawing unwanted experiences into your existence.

Our beliefs are usually attached to things we know. We rely on memory to help recall information based on these so-called known facts. True belief gives way to powerful forces that create your every desire, but true belief should not necessarily be based upon things you know. The known is based on your past experiences and does not allow for things yet to be. All things known are of past cognitive conditioning. Even with all things known, the constant movement of energy creates opportunities to experience something completely different each and every time, moment to moment. Remember:

1. Believing is an inner knowing and confidence.
2. True belief is absent of fear and doubt.
3. Emotions carry your belief—always.

DETACH FROM PAST EXPERIENCE

If you live in the moment, every experience will be new and exciting. You can choose to walk a path paved by your own creation.

1. Detach from past conditioning. You can choose to detach from a belief or from others' experiences by removing your own personal history. Doing so allows each and every experience to be new and fresh, not cluttered with any preconceived negative thought vibration.

2. Recondition your thinking in any way you desire. Removing your personal history is a great way to allow for a new experience while walking a perceived path you believe to be familiar. This type of reconditioning develops a belief system based exclusively on your own experiences, in the moment, not those of others.

3. Periodically challenge and question your belief system. Make sure your beliefs are your own, not plagiarized from elsewhere. When it comes to thought creation, it is important not to import past beliefs and habits.

SUMMARY

If you think about something hard or long enough, you will create a belief. Words are just labels until you back them up with belief. You create intention with belief, which is the driving force of intention and any creation. Holding a belief is the surest way to allow the Law of Attraction to bring experiences into your existence. It also brings you into harmonious vibration with what you desire.

An endless field of possibility, hope, and abundance is tied to belief and is limited only by you and your attachment to your history. The universe can create and bring to you only experience based on your belief, which begs the question: what do you believe?

Everyone that asketh receiveth, and he that seeketh findeth. All things are possible to him that believeth. —Matthew 7:8

So I tell you, whatever you ask for in prayer believe that you have received it, and it will be yours. —Matthew 21:22

VII

Allow, Don't Resist

Resistance is not allowing what the universe shows us. When we resist, we stop creation.——- *Unknown*

Allowing is the opposite of resisting. Allowing sets us free. It is the willingness to accept that which comes into your experience without resistance. This does not mean you have to continue to settle for the outcome of a particular creational experience or embrace a situation that is not to your liking. It simply means to allow what is, without passing judgment and labeling, and to begin focusing on what you want, if in fact your current experience is not what you desire.

By allowing what is, and not resisting it, you flow with the current of the universe and become aware and present-minded. So many times we use words such as no, but, can't, don't, shouldn't, won't, if only—to name a few. All of these words offer resistance to what is and give way to negative energy vibrations. The more you push against what you don't want, the more you will create what you don't want.

Our society is a macro version of resisting. Over and over we read or hear about the "War on: terror, drugs, gangs, illiteracy, cancer, etc." Although people mean well by doing this, they do not understand how the Law of Attraction matches them with their energies. Again, we must focus on what we want, not on what we do not want. Once we focus as a collective consciousness on peace, health, knowledge, and abundance, we will start to create and share in a world that does not need to push against anything. That which is undesired will no longer exist.

Remembering that you create every experience or situation you encounter will help reinforce that anything at any time can be changed, or created, to your liking and acceptance. Sometimes, though, you may be so focused on a grain of sand that you lose sight of the entire ecosystem. You don't always understand what is, and why it is happening to you, but you can be sure you created it with a single thought. The ever-expanding universe is answering your thoughts, and every one will be created if you allow it to be.

Understand, however, that just because you imagined the path for your desire to appear does not mean the universe of creation will always follow that course. Allowing also sheds light on not knowing how desires might arrive. To truly allow, you cannot wonder about the "how." That is for the universe to handle, and it will.

There are numerous dynamics involved when the creational universe manifests your desire or want into your experience. This is why "Be careful what you ask for" and maintaining your desired vibrational output are so important. If you move in and out of a particular vibration regarding an intended desire, you start a new vibration of creation each time you waver. You begin to believe that your desires are not being answered. But the truth of the matter is all your desires are being answered. You are simply not aware of your vibrational output. For each and every new emotional change and vibrational output, the process starts over again, which leads you to believe your desires are going unanswered.

For example, imagine you want to create a new home for your family. You set your desire into motion by expressing it. You create a mental image, and once you have a mental image, you take that image and bring it alive in your mind by visualizing yourself enjoying your new home. You feel the excitement and you feel all the positive emotions associated with your new home. You believe without a doubt that this house is yours. You see yourself from the end point of your desire and watch it unfold towards you.

Doing this and holding your image raises your vibration to that of positive creation, and the process begins. You continue to hold this created vibration for a few months until you lose sight of it, and disbelief starts to set in because you have yet to see your desire manifest. This disbelief causes the positive vibrational output to change to one of lacking. At this point, you start a chain reaction in the vibrational output of creation. The universe now shifts to bring to you your new vibrational output, the one of lacking and not having the house of your desires. You have just created your new vibrational creation—no house. After a period of time, you realign with the belief of being able to create the house of your desires again and the whole process begins anew.

Without prejudice, the universe will create for us. Sometimes our self-imagined time frame is different from what we expect or want it to be. It's important to remember that the universe does not operate on a clock. It has no time or space boundaries. The creative universe does not occupy the same mind-made boundaries or limitations we have imposed upon ourselves. This is why we sometimes give up on our ability to create our experience. To overcome this, be aware of your impatience and your fluctuating variances of vibrational frequency.

In the example, extenuating circumstances were taking place and being taken care of in order for the created desire to manifest. Do not resist what is. Maintain your energy vibration so the creative universe can align your vibration with that of a like vibration. You have to believe, without doubt, that no matter what circumstances or situations appear, you will manifest the object or experience of your desires. And if, for some reason, an experience appears that is uncomfortable or not to your liking, you don't have to resist it. Just check to see if your emotions and/or beliefs still match your desire. From there you can make the appropriate adjustments to your thinking and belief system to help facilitate your desired outcome.

ALLEVIATING PHYSICAL AND EMOTIONAL PAIN

Resisting is not associated only with the physical realm of material creation. Allowing is an essential element in any type of creation, including physical and emotional pain. Remember, you create every single experience you have. This also includes physical pain, emotional pain, and illness. Resisting can increase the amount of physical and emotional pain you experience.

Physical and emotional pain can be alleviated or increased dramatically, depending on the amount of resisting you choose to create or the amount of non-resistance you choose to give. As long as you acknowledge the pain or illness for what it is, either emotional or physical, and do not allow it to become who you are, you will lessen its time in your experience.

CONTROL YOUR PAIN

The next time you experience some type of pain or illness, physical or emotional:

1. Try to relax through it completely.
2. Be aware of your tightening muscles, or tensing up or any repeating negative dialogues in your mind.
3. Do not give attention to or focus upon your current experience.
4. Take deep breaths and simply tell yourself at the moment of discomfort, "My mind and body are strong. At this time I feel the loving spirit of God and only God. Thank you for my continued health and well-being. I feel good now."
5. Repeat this as many times as you feel necessary.
6. Erase your personal history regarding your pain, illness, or emotional past. Do not keep it alive by talking to others and telling them how bad you feel or felt at one time. Remember, by focusing on what you do not want, you create more of what you do not want.

By following these steps, you are not focusing on or owning the situation. You are not resisting, but rather are allowing the natural course of the universe to flow and remove your pain. You can see and feel the amazing pure love and natural healing of God Energy flowing through the physical experience of your spiritual being. You will witness this self-induced healing, and you will experience freedom from your discomfort as long as you believe without resistance.

SUMMARY

Allow what you ask for through the practice of non-resistance. Allowing works only in complete acceptance of what is. For you to bring forth the manifestation of your desires you must relinquish all fear and doubt. True allowing and non-resistance resonate because of a belief and faith in God Energy and your connection to it.

Your knowing that all is possible with a simple belief gives way to the allowing. There is a purpose and order to everything, which has no choice but to show up in your experience through the path of least resistance.

Resistance is based on fear, allowing is based on belief.——Unknown

VIII

Detachment

Detachment believes in universal abundance. ——— *Unknown*

There is no reason to ever become attached to anything, when you truly understand how it arrived. ——— *Unknown*

Detachment is an easy but often misunderstood principle when creating your desires and shaping your experiences. People often say that detachment is a contradiction to desires and wants, which is absolutely untrue. Detachment basically means to release your sense of self from the desired outcome. Our purpose in this physical realm is to learn how to create joy and happiness and experience our lives to the fullest. Releasing the self from a desired outcome actually has two aspects: (1) detach from how your created desire will arrive into your experience and (2) do not become identified with the object or experience of your created desire.

The first aspect we will cover is detaching from the "how will this created desire arrive into my experience?" This aspect parallels the allowing of what is, as covered in the previous chapter. Again, allowing is the non-resistance of experiences and situations that are drawn to your experience at the present moment.

ALLOWING YOUR CREATED DESIRE TO FLOW TO YOU

The first aspect of detachment is allowing your created desire to flow to you by means of God Energy, not by a forced path the limited boundaries of your mind create. This aspect encompasses the allowing of your desires and experiences to appear and continues without your worrying about how they might arrive.

The detachment process or element is linked to true belief. True belief is the knowing that something greater than ourselves—God Energy—has the ability, without fail, to bring into our experience that which we desire.

To detach, you must believe and understand that just because you cannot imagine how your desire will manifest into your experience does not mean it cannot or will not happen. You need to detach from any preconceived notions or doubts and believe that all is possible, even if you do not understand at the present moment. You do not have to understand the universe of God Energy's order and organization for it to create your desires. Many times things happen or circumstances present themselves without our knowing how, but that did not affect our emotional response. The truth of the matter is, how it will be will always be the work of the universe. Do not worry about how, even when what you're seeking seems impossible.

To give an example, my ten-year-old daughter had an undying desire to go to Hawaii for about two years. All my wife and I heard was, "I want to go to Hawaii, when are we going to go?" Any opportunity she found to ask, she did. "Dad, can we go to Hawaii this year for vacation?" "Dad, how about taking me out of school for a week and taking me to Hawaii?"

She was truly relentless with her desire to go to Hawaii. One day I sat her down and told her to write down her desire and place it in a box we would call her magic box. I told her to think about her desire, act as if she had already received it, and believe it would happen. At that time she said, "Dad, how is that going to get me to Hawaii?" I told her to just give it a try, and believe. I also told her to look in her magic box as often as she wanted, think about being in Hawaii, and visualize what she would like to do while she was in Hawaii. After some mild resistance and disbelief she started to compile pictures from magazines and started her own creation process.

About two weeks into her creation training I received a call from my sister who lives in Virginia. During our conversation she told me the U.S. Navy was transferring her husband to Hawaii in about six months.

At that moment I knew what had happened. The sheer delight on my daughter's face when I told her about the conversation was priceless. She expressed her joy to me in two ways. One was the fact that she was actually going to get a chance to go to Hawaii, and two was the realization in her eyes that she did in fact create it. The true beauty of it all was the fact that she had no idea how it might happen. She just believed that it would. The true power of her own ability was witnessed again when a few weeks later she was told by her mom, who she alternates a residence with, that she had scheduled a Hawaiian vacation for their family to go on. My daughter actually created two direct avenues that allowed her to experience her desire. This was possible in her mind without the knowing or the worry of how. Because her belief was so strong, she was not aware that she was implementing the rule of detachment.

When you lock your mind on something or try to force a path for it to happen, you constrict many possible solutions from presenting themselves. At that time, I had no idea when my wife and I would be able to take her to Hawaii. It was just one of those things that wasn't on my priority list at the moment, but all of a sudden my daughter's desire announced, "I'm here!"

DO NOT BECOME IDENTIFIED WITH YOUR CREATED DESIRE

The second aspect of detachment is to make sure you do not become identified with your created desire or experience. Sometimes people associate their created desire with what they are rather than identifying themselves as separate from their manifestation. We have all seen someone at some time become so consumed with their possessions or their title that they actually forget who they are, that they are a spiritual being experiencing a physical realm.

There are some people who have to have designer labels on their clothes, or people who look down upon others because of the car they drive or the house they live in. Sometimes the only things these people talk about are their possessions or their job title, as if that is who they are. They become upset if an item or personal possession gets broken or marred.

People who have an attachment to material things or who seek their identity through physical form react negatively because of a true sense of loss in their reality. This type of personality usually puts greater importance on material things than their families and others. Unfortunately, some of these spiritual beings never become aware of the fact that they have unlimited ability to create that which they desire in abundance, over and over again, if they chose.

THE WORLD OF PHYSICAL FORM

The world of physical form is here for you to explore and enjoy. It is your innate ability and your gift to create and experience your creations as you walk this path of incarnation. Everyone has the same ability and opportunity to create from this world of nothingness and should do so, as long as you understand its true nature and as long as you don't seek your identity from within the world of form.

We have all heard someone at one time or another say, "As soon as I get my new _____ (fill in the blank), I will be happy." The problem with this statement is, that time will never come. You can't seek your true happiness from the attainment of a material form or goal. It cannot happen. You might have a brief moment of contentment, but over time your perception of form ages and changes and that keeps you searching for a sense of happiness over and over in the world of form. You will always find yourself dissatisfied when you perceive you need something to be bigger or better than what you have, to keep you happy or at peace.

We cannot find happiness or peace within while looking outside of ourselves. If an object were able to bring true peace and contentment to your life, you would never want or desire anything more to complete your sense of happiness. It would already be there, in the item of your desired creation. It is senseless to believe in or buy into the notion that the world of form can bring any sort of true, lasting happiness. This attachment to physical form is a true mental frailty. Yet at one time or another everyone has engaged in this state of mental delusion.

Take a look at the world around you, the world you created and your so-called possessions. Chances are, each item you have in your home brought you some form of short-lived happiness at the time it arrived into your experience. It might be a car, furniture, clothing, novelties, art, or accessories. It doesn't matter. Try to remember how you felt when you acquired any one of those items. Does it feel the same now as it did when you first bought it? Most likely the joy you once felt with any particular item has diminished or mellowed considerably. That's just the way it is. The world of form is for you to experience. It is not a means for you to find yourself or acquire true joy and happiness.

There is nothing wrong with creating new and wonderful things in your life to have fun and play with. You are meant to do that. The problem lies in the attachment to whatever you create, the belief that this new creation adds something to who you are or who you believe you are. You can determine if you are attached to any realm of the world of form by paying attention to the emotions you feel when you lose something or it becomes damaged. If you are not attached to it, you cannot experience any negative emotion if you lose it.

Expressing, or better put, choosing to attach a negative emotion to the loss of a created physical form reinforces your belief that you can't acquire it or create it again. It's the lack of belief that will keep you in a neutral state of creation. Remember, the key to creating your life is the belief that you can do it, and if this belief is truly part of your foundation, you will never grieve the loss from anything in the world of form.

It is not a bad thing to create possessions like a big, beautiful house, expensive cars, or designer clothing, or have a title you worked hard to achieve. All of these are great examples of what can be created if you so desire. Just do not associate yourself with these items. Don't create a fancy car just because you want your neighbors to see you in it. Don't create an expensive house just to make someone jealous or envious. Your creations are little miracles that are for you to enjoy and experience.

Be careful not to allow your ego to take control and change your vibration. By attaching your ego to anything you create, you are promoting scarcity, not universal abundance, in your life. Your ego tells you that these things need to be protected at all cost. Your ego tells you that you will not be able to create another car or home if this one goes away. Your ego fills you with insecurity if you don't dress appropriately.

On the other hand, if you truly believe in the ability to create your desire and wants, you have no reason to attach yourself to anything. You truly believe in the abundance of God Energy and your ability to create your desires at any time. Detachment only knows abundance. It does not know scarcity. If you really think about it, at no time in your physical life do you truly own anything. It doesn't matter what auto loan or mortgage you paid off. In the grand scheme of things you are just temporarily leasing these things. If you did own your possessions, you could load up a moving truck and take your stuff with you when you no longer need your body. But as an old friend of mine once said, "You'll never see a luggage rack on a hearse."

PROMOTE ABUNDANCE

1. Detach your sense of personal-self from your created desire. Attachment to your desires creates a vibration of lacking.
2. You will never find sustained happiness from any physical form. Happiness is the journey, not the destination.

3. You can determine your level of attachment to anything by becoming aware of the emotions you feel towards it if it were to go away.
4. Only your ego needs to identify with labels. Ego-attachment promotes scarcity.
5. Truly believing in your ability to create promotes abundance. Create, have fun and detach. There is only abundance in the source of God Energy.

SUMMARY

Creating and experiencing is the name of the game here, and you should truly enjoy and embrace every created desire and experience. Release any attachment to the "how" and release any self-attachment to your creations. Just enjoy them.

In the realm of God Energy anything is possible and can be replicated with great abundance, if you so choose. Don't constrict the great natural flow of God Energy with thoughts of scarcity or disbelief. Just believe and allow it. Then watch as the life you created blossoms into your experience.

Seek refuge in the attitude of detachment and you will amass the wealth of spiritual awareness. Those who are motivated only by the desire, for the fruits of their actions are miserable, for they are constantly anxious about the results of what they do.

Action motivated by expectation is doomed before it begins. Action without expectation never fails to open the doorway to infinity. We are the authors of our expectations; it is time to stop writing.
— Bhagavad-Gita 2:49-50

IX

Just Be

Listen or thy tongue will keep thee deaf. —*American Indian Proverb*

Prayer is when we talk to God; Meditation is when we listen to God. —*Unknown*

"Just be." This statement is probably the easiest aspect of creating your daily life experience if you allow it to just be. To just be does not require any special training or knowledge. The only thing required is that you do nothing.

There is no need for thought or action of any kind at this level of experience. The key is to become comfortable in the silence and purity of God Energy. This is where perspective, desire, want, energy vibration, imagination, visualization, believing, allowing, and detachment all reside. There is no place for ego or fear here, just pure silence and a knowing that does not require thought or acknowledgement. When you allow yourself to just be, you remove judgments, labels, concern, worry, fear, resentment, jealousy, doubt, disbelief, need for protection, assumptions, control, envy, discontent, unhappiness, sadness, or any negative-labeled energy vibration.

When you allow yourself to just be, you are acknowledging and allowing your expression to resonate to that which you are, God Energy. By allowing this, you unlock the doors of every desire and experience you want to create. One way to do this is through meditation. Meditation is a practice that allows you to enter into that creative, silent realm of pure God Energy and just be.

Sometimes the word meditation conjures up images of robed holy men with long beards, sitting with their eyes closed in what appears to be an uncomfortable position, and chanting or making vibronic sounds. Although this can be a true image and practice to some, the essence of meditation is just "being." It does not have to incorporate this stereotypical image for you to enter into it or practice it.

MEDITATE AND JUST BE

Many of us have become so attached to our physical self-expression that we do not remember our true essence of stillness. When you begin to meditate, you might experience what appear to be wild and random thoughts that zip in and out of your mind like a plague of locusts. Do not let this frustrate you if it happens. We have somewhere between 65,000 and 85,000 thoughts each and every day. It is normal for your mind to be active with abundant thoughts—most of which are the same ones repeated over and over.

Ego-controlled thoughts repeat in our heads the majority of the time. Other thoughts include labels, judgments, fears, dialogue projections, the past, the future, and all the negative thoughts of which we are unaware. Some of these thoughts are strange, abstract concepts that are difficult to categorize, but continue to swirl around in your mind without effort.

It might appear that the ego continually conjures up many of your extra, needless thoughts to justify its existence and confirm you need it. An important point then is to learn how to think and react beyond your ego-conscious mind.

If you learn to become aware of your thoughts and believe you have control of the experiences that show up in your life, you will silence your mind and your ego with the same wand. If you truly believe, you will have no need for extra dialogue or needless thoughts.

GETTING STARTED

1. Find a comfortable position to relax where you can be still.
2. Sit, lie down, stand, lean against something, or even assume an uncomfortable position if you like.
3. Relax in a position that allows you to remain comfortable and enter into stillness. No thought is needed here, just be.
4. There is no need to force anything at this point, no need to think about or do anything.

5. Just be. It is as simple as closing your eyes and relaxing into the stillness.

At first, this may be challenging because of your mind's inner chatter. Do not allow this to deter you from practicing your reconnection to God Energy.

6. Gently push extra chatter and random thoughts away when you become aware of them.
7. Do not hold onto them, but rather allow them to leave as easily as they entered.
8. Just be and remain still in the mind. Do not react. 20 to 30 minutes a day is all it takes to reconnect to your true self. With time and practice, the process of meditation will become easier, to the point it is truly effortless.

It is not necessary to enter into meditation with thoughts, not even with the desire or want you are contemplating and creating. This aspect of the creation process goes beyond creating the life you want to experience. This is the process that allows you to reconnect with your true essence, the true essence of God Energy.

By entering into the silence and stillness of creative God Energy, you allow the universal forces of energy to flow naturally and without resistance through your physical expression and experience. You are aligning and resonating a vibrational match to God Energy that, in turn, allows you to become a direct conduit of creational energy. Knowing is in the stillness and silence of God Energy. Through this knowing, you have belief, and through this belief, all creation happens. Meditation is the way for you to reconnect and experience all the beauty in the stillness, the silence, the love, and the wellness of pure God Energy.

At times you may enter into the expression of meditation without being aware of it. You silence your mind and just be when you listen to music, walk in nature, watch a sunset, stare into a campfire, star gaze, fly a kite, watch waves crash onto a beach, watch birds fly, watch fish swim, perform a hobby, listen to the wind, drive a car, swim, ski, or engage in any activity that allows you to just be. Allowing yourself to just be in any chosen activity without resistance through your thoughts and beliefs allows you to reconnect to and experience pure, creative God Energy.

SUMMARY

Make meditation a desirable daily habit. It should never feel like a chore. Allow the reconnection to God Energy to bring a sense of joy to your heart, because your true essence is in that realm of joy.

Step into the realm of the unknown and fear not. Everything you think you know and everything you think you do not know is there, in the silence, in the stillness, in the love, in the wellness of pure, creative God Energy.

When we 'think not' the presence of the all becomes apparent in the ensuing silence. —Matthew 24:44

Spend more time alone everyday, for our purpose in life is to be happy and reconnect. —Unknown

Be still and know that I am God. —Psalm 46:10

Just sit there right now, don't do a thing, just rest, for your separation from God, from Love, is the hardest work in this world. — Hafiz, The Gift

X

Putting It All Together

The sum of the parts is equal to the whole. —Unknown

Creating your life is about creating yourself and the path you choose to follow. Moment to moment, the life you live is a continuous reflection of how you think and feel. Albert Einstein once said, "We can't solve problems by using the same kind of thinking we used when we created them."

Only you can control your thoughts and the feelings attached to your thoughts, and thus control your experiences. Believe that all is possible, and all that is possible will be.

Creating your life starts with a single thought tied to a strong, positive emotion that says, "More is always available for me to experience and enjoy." A single thought can literally move a mountain if it is allowed to be. Turn your attention inward and become aware, for every single thought and belief you carry has the power to positively create your direct experience or negatively alter and challenge your direct experience. The choice, always, is yours.

The reconditioning of thought awareness is not a difficult task but it does require practice. We have all heard at one time or another, "If at first you don't succeed, try, try again."

Like learning a new language or a new skill, the more you practice, the better you will become. Allow the understanding of this creative knowledge to embrace your essence and saturate, for once you understand it, this creative law will gently embrace you with an abundance of peace, love, and joy.

SUMMARY: IMAGINE, BELIEVE AND BE

1. **Develop thought awareness to gain perspective and learn to think in the right mind.** Once you become aware of your thoughts, you are directly accountable for every experience you encounter. You can no longer blame others for why you think something went wrong or for why you believe you lack something. Change your thoughts and you change your life.

2. **Be careful what you think and feel about.** Pay close attention to your true thought focus and/or the belief you are generating when asking for something. Without an emotional belief system, a thought is just a thought. It's when you attach thought to emotion, when you genuinely feel your thoughts, you learn to create from a force greater than that of $E = MC^2$.

3. **High and low energy, after all, it's just energy.** Realizing that it is just energy allows you to understand that anything can be changed. The fact that everything is energy tells us that no one entity has sole entitlement to this unlimited abundant source. You have the ability to shape your life exactly the way you want by using this creative force.

4. **Raise your energy level and realize the benefits of the Law of Attraction.** The Law of Attraction shows us "that which is like itself is drawn to itself." Simply put, change your energy vibration to that of an energy vibration you want to experience. You cannot create health if you think or feel ill. You cannot create abundance if you believe you are lacking what you want. You can receive only what you vibrate as or what you are and give.

5. **Use your imagination and the art of visualization to allow the boundless and the unknown to come alive with simple thought and belief.** Don't be afraid to dream big applies here. Whatever the mind can conceive, it can achieve. Never set limits. Limits are the result of a weak belief system. Allow your dreams and desires to come alive with vivid color and great emotion while you visualize them. The more you feel it, the quicker you will live it.

6. **Have faith in the unknown by internalizing "Believing is seeing."** You will truly see it, when you truly believe it. Belief + Anticipation = Manifestation. Believing "as if" brings everything alive in the mind's eye and brings you one step closer to living the life you created.

7.   **Allow, don't resist.** Do not resist the natural flow of God Energy. Resistance is the non-belief of what could be. Just because you might not be witness to your desires does not mean they are not on their way. The universe will form the path for any creative thought, and true allowing paves the way. Allowing what is and what will be is seated in an unbending belief that all of your desires and wants will be, without fail. Allow and accept what is. Do not push against what is but allow it to be as it presents itself. By pushing against what is, you create more of what you are pushing against. Allow what is, and focus upon what you want. That is true creation.

8.   **Detach and have faith in your ability to create anything you desire through God Energy, and do not worry about the outcome.** True detachment is the innate understanding that what you desire already is. True detachment is an evoked self-freedom that relies upon belief and knowledge. Without the burden or worry of how, and with a true knowing of what is, you empower your knowledge and ability of self-creation. Relax. Know that it is on its way.

9.   **Just be.** This is the reconnection to your true self. Complete acceptance of who we are requires plugging back into and becoming aware of the pure spiritual essence of your being. By allowing yourself to reconnect to a realm that is non-judgmental and knows only unconditional love and well-being, brings to awareness a knowledge that we are all connected to one thing, God Energy. "Just be" allows for the reconnection to what you truly seek in your physical form and what you truly are—joy and peace. Resonate to the true vibration of God Energy through the Law of Attraction and you will create an endless source of positive God Energy to create through and "just be."

10. **Treat yourself and your life like the child you would love.**
11. **Believe in every thing that is not, and believe that it can be.** You create each and every experience through your thoughts and beliefs. Remember, it is your emotions that determine your belief system. If you can believe, it can be. Don't limit yourself to the known. You are a timeless and boundless energy being with unlimited potential and ability.

Live your life in a perpetual state of gratitude. Give thanks to anything and everything you want more of in your life. Know that the Law of Attraction is working at all times, regardless of your known or unknown understanding of this powerful, innate universal law.

Put your thoughts forward. Imagine, Believe, Be—and your world will become your known and desired creation.

Although you appear in earthly form, your essence is pure Consciousness. You are the fearless guardian of Divine Light …

When you lose all sense of self the bonds of a thousand chains will vanish. Lose yourself completely … Why are you so enchanted by this world when a mine of gold lies within you? Open your eyes and come. Return to the root of your own soul. ——- Jalaluddin Rumi

Focused on a single leaf, we lose sight of the trees, the forest, the earth, the sky, the One. —Unknown

Breinigsville, PA USA
14 January 2010
230789BV00001B/4/A